INTO Wild Madagascar

BLACKBIRCH®
PRESS

THOMSON

™

GALE

San Diego • Detroit • New York • San Francisco • Cleveland • New Haven, Conn. • Waterville, Maine • London • Munich

THOMSON
—*—
GALE

LIBRARY OF CONGRESS CATALOGING-IN-PUBLICATION DATA

Into wild Madagascar / Elaine Pascoe, book editor.
    p. cm. — (The Jeff Corwin experience)
Based on an episode from a Discovery Channel program hosted by Jeff Corwin.
Summary: Television personality Jeff Corwin takes the reader on an expedition of Madagascar, a large island off the east coast of Africa, and introduces some of the unusual wildlife found there.
Includes bibliographical references (p.) and index.
  ISBN 1-56711-855-0 (alk. paper) — ISBN 1-4103-0174-5 (pbk. : alk. paper)
  1. Madagascar—Description and travel—Juvenile literature. 2. Natural history—Madagascar—Juvenile literature. 3. Wilderness areas—Madagascar—Juvenile literature. 4. Corwin, Jeff—Journeys—Madagascar—Juvenile literature. [1. Zoology—Madagascar. 2. Madagascar—Description and travel. 3. Corwin, Jeff.] I. Pascoe, Elaine. II. Corwin, Jeff. III. Series.

DT469.M28I57 2004
591.9691—dc21
                          2003009276

Printed in China
10 9 8 7 6 5 4 3 2 1

E ver since I was a kid, I dreamed about traveling around the world, visiting exotic places, and seeing all kinds of incredible animals. And now, guess what? That's exactly what I get to do!

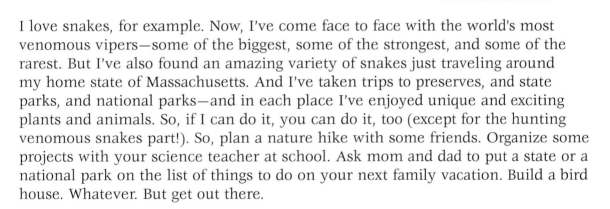

Yes, I am incredibly lucky. But, you don't have to have your own television show on Animal Planet to go off and explore the natural world around you. I mean, I travel to Madagascar and the Amazon and all kinds of really cool places—but I don't need to go that far to see amazing wildlife up close. In fact, I can find thousands of incredible critters right here, in my own backyard—or in my neighbor's yard (he does get kind of upset when he finds me crawling around in the bushes, though). The point is, no matter where you are, there's fantastic stuff to see in nature. All you have to do is look.

I love snakes, for example. Now, I've come face to face with the world's most venomous vipers—some of the biggest, some of the strongest, and some of the rarest. But I've also found an amazing variety of snakes just traveling around my home state of Massachusetts. And I've taken trips to preserves, and state parks, and national parks—and in each place I've enjoyed unique and exciting plants and animals. So, if I can do it, you can do it, too (except for the hunting venomous snakes part!). So, plan a nature hike with some friends. Organize some projects with your science teacher at school. Ask mom and dad to put a state or a national park on the list of things to do on your next family vacation. Build a bird house. Whatever. But get out there.

As you read through these pages and look at the photos, you'll probably see how jazzed I get when I come face to face with beautiful animals. That's good. I want you to feel that excitement. And I want you to remember that—even if you don't have your own TV show—you can still experience the awesome beauty of nature almost anywhere you go—any day of the week. I only hope that I can help bring that awesome power and beauty a little closer to you. Enjoy!

Best Wishes!

Jeff

INTO *Wild* *Madagascar*

In the Indian Ocean, off the southeast coast of Africa, is an island that time has forgotten. This beautiful island has been isolated from the mainland for millions of years. It's crawling with reptiles and other bizarre and wonderful creatures—an evolutionary explosion of wildlife. Get ready to see creatures you've never seen before as we explore Madagascar, the fourth largest island in the world.

I'm Jeff Corwin.
Welcome to Madagascar.

The mysterious island of Madagascar seems to be filled with prehistoric-looking creatures. Well, they're not exactly dinosaurs; but they are lizards, and there are lots of them—including more varieties of chameleons than you'll see anywhere else on the planet.

This island is chameleon central!

Ahh, look at this beautiful rain forest.

We're starting our exploration in Montagne D'Ambre National Park, which has more than forty thousand acres of pristine rain forest. And right away we have an amazing discovery, one of the largest chameleons in the world. This is Oustalet's chameleon. Look at the way he's built. He's got an armored-looking, arrow-shaped head, with a large crest that tells us he's a male. Males are larger than females, growing almost two feet in length.

Check this chameleon out!

Chameleons have very bizarre, strange-looking feet. Look at those toes—they're fused. Basically, two toes have fused in one bundle, and the other three have fused in a second bundle. These are called zygodactylic feet, and they're perfect tools for climbing.

The eyes of this beast are amazing. Each eye moves individually, so a chameleon has the extraordinary ability to look ahead with one eye while the other eye rotates and looks behind.

Look at these toes...

...and eyes that can look in two different directions!

A chameleon's color reflects its mood.

What do you think this color means?

Chameleons are very emotional creatures, and they show their emotions with their colors. They have colors for rage, for conquest, and for sexuality when they're in their reproductive stages.

What makes Madagascar unique is that this island has been isolated from the rest of the world for millions of years. You can think
of this place as one great evolutionary experiment that's gone wild.
Many of the creatures that live here, in fact 90 percent of them, are
found nowhere else in the world. And each year, believe it or not,
the people of Madagascar discover five new species.

Look at this frog. It's a tomato frog, a female. Females are nearly
the double the size of males, and they really bring home what it is
to be tomato—plump, fleshy, red. Years ago, there were plenty of
these frogs, but today
they're starting to disap-
pear. I do believe they're
very close to being listed
as an endangered species.

You see why
they call these
tomato frogs?

Many scientists consid-
er creatures like this to be
indicator species, species
that give us a clue to the
health of an ecosystem.
That's because these frogs
are extremely sensitive to
changes in the ecosystem,

even to air quality. They survive through a process called cutaneous respiration, which means they not only breathe with their lungs but also rely on air that passes through their skin. That's why I'm very careful when I hold this frog. If I hold her too much, if I have any salts or soap or chemicals on my hand, they'll pass right from my hand into the bloodstream of this animal. I don't want that, so I'm just being extremely careful.

These creatures breathe through their skin.

As with all the amphibians, these creatures don't have any true teeth or claws. But they do have a great defense. When a predator decides to gobble this animal down its throat, it's going to get a nasty surprise. Tomato frogs secrete a gluey, thick substance that gums up when it hits saliva.

Tomato frogs have an excellent defense against predators—they taste awful!

It coats the tongue, teeth, and palate and creates a very nasty dining experience. A creature bites and then quickly releases the frog when it gets a nasty taste like that.

This frog actually hopped right in my mouth. But, clearly, she recognized me as a lover of frogs and did not secrete anything but a nice wet kiss.

Dinosaurs used to roam here.

Some truly extraordinary dinosaur fossils have been discovered here in Madagascar, including the oldest one ever found, about 225 million years in age. But the wildlife that's around today is no less extraordinary.

This is a special kind of mammal.

Look what we have right in front of us. Nothing like a dinosaur—we have a female tenrec with her babies. She's foraging around looking for food, and her babies are scattered all about. Tenrecs belong to the order of mammals we call insectivores, and that sure is a clue to what

Small guys, but sharp teeth.

Is that the cutest tenrec baby you've ever seen?

these animals eat. They have very sensitive whiskers that actually detect the slight vibrations of potential insect prey. Then they grab onto the prey with extremely sharp teeth, munch it up, and swallow it whole. A little guy like this baby can swallow a worm twice its size. These creatures have a very fast metabolism, so they have to continuously feed themselves to keep their energy up.

Tenrecs are an ancient group of mammals. They've been living on this planet for millions of years, practically unchanged. And before this little one gets separated from its family, I'm going to send it back.

Wow! Here's a bunch of crowned lemurs.

Wow—right above our heads, we've got a troop of crowned lemurs, members of a very ancient and bizarre group of primates. Lemurs are prosimians, primitive primates. They are unique to Madagascar, and there are more than thirty different kinds.

These are another kind of lemurs called ring-tailed lemurs.

See the "V"?

There are lemurs in all these trees.

These crowned lemurs have an orange V-shaped pattern on the top of their heads, which gives them their name.

There's a female about fifteen feet away from my hand, just looking down, and behind her is one of her offspring. Actually lemurs are all over these branches. When you first look, you don't see anything, but when you look more closely they appear. These animals are so cool, with their long tails. They're quick and agile, moving through the trees as if they were dancing.

Panther chameleons are incredible.

Whoa—check this lizard out. This is *furcifer pardalis*, the panther chameleon. Both male and female panther chameleons have vivid, beautiful coloration. There's a ribbon of blue in the center, some green, and bars of red and brown.

Not only is this one of the largest of the chameleons in Madagascar, but he makes himself even larger. This fellow's feeling

He's puffing up to try to scare me.

That fleshy tongue is a lot longer than it looks.

a little threatened. He doesn't know what to make of us. He wants us to think that he's big and bad, and he does that by puffing up with air and extending his chin pouch, displaying those bright colors. He's larger than life. He looks fierce. But most of it is a bluff; he is not dangerous.

Look inside that mouth, and you can see the fleshy tip of his tongue, half an inch or a quarter of an inch in length. But that is just the very tip. The tongue can instantly spray out, like a party favor, more than the length of this creature's body. The tongue zips out, grabs an insect, and pulls it back in. That's how this creature eats.

In this land that time forgot, there are sixty different species of chameleons. Each is unique and has followed its own pathway of survival. Some are living in the forest canopy. Some are living on the forest floor. Some of them are huge. Some of them are as small as a matchstick.

World's smallest chameleon...

...the Brookesia minima.

Look at this fantastic creature. I feel like I'm looking at a puppet created by a human being—but this is a live, breathing chameleon. It's the smallest species of chameleon in the world, *Brookesia minima*. Typically you'll find this lizard no more than two or three feet above the forest floor. It's not a great climber, and it likes to stay low and close to the leaf litter. Its body is much bigger than its limbs are. It's absolutely twiglike in appearance And what is extraordinary about this animal is that even though it is basically one knuckle in length, it's all chameleon, perfectly designed. You can see those little eyes rolling about in its head.

Yes! Found a snake!

A tree boa.

Madagascar is a Garden of Eden, a place where one fascinating discovery follows another. Just take a moment and check out the design of this creature. It's one of the few species of constrictors living on the island of Madagascar. And this is a spectacular species. It's the *Sanzinia boa*, or Madagascar tree boa.

This snake is not venomous, but he's got some pretty long teeth. If I move slowly, I may work him out of his tree and onto

Tree boas are constrictors.

my hand. He's a very strong snake—this is a creature that uses squeezing as a way to survive. Right now he's using those powerful muscles to squeeze his way up a branch. When it's time for him to eat, he will squeeze his prey in a deadly hug called constriction. This animal eats everything—birds, rodents, even things that are painful to swallow, like tenrecs or hedgehogs. He even eats primates, like small lemurs. When he's hunting, he sits completely still outside the cavity of a tree, perfectly camouflaged with his surroundings, and waits. And when the little lemur sticks its head out—swoosh! —the snake grabs on.

You might think chameleons are the ultimate in the art of protective coloration, but there are other creatures living here that take camouflage to a whole new level. Here's a little challenge for you. Let your eyes quickly scan this vine and tell

Lizards and chameleons everywhere...

...especially in trees.

Super camouflage!

Look at that tail.

me if you can see anything. If you saw a lizard, you're right. If you didn't see a lizard, you weren't looking hard enough.

This is one of the many different types of leaf-tailed geckos in Madagascar. I have to say that it has some of the best camouflage I have ever seen. Just look at that tail—you can see why it's called the leaf-tailed gecko.

I'm really just blown away by the camouflage. Not only is this animal equipped with shades of different coloration in his skin to blend in with wood and bark, but he also has some mimicry. He has what look to be little clumps of lichen and moss on his body. That looks like lichen on top of his head. If you look along his body, you see what seem to be little patches of moss. This is the zenith of nature—for a creature such as this lizard to evolve a pattern in its skin that so closely mirrors the habitat around it.

Here's something else that's amazing. This creature does not have eyelids. Instead, it has a windshield wiper—its tongue. It actually can clean its eyeballs, sweep off debris, with its tongue!

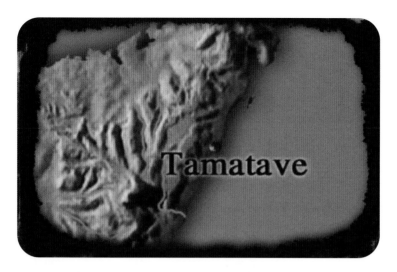

Tamatave

There's one now!

Next we're off to a town called Tamatave, on the eastern coast of the island. We're going to see some creatures unlike any others in the world.

We're at Park Ivoloina, a wildlife sanctuary and biological park of eight hundred acres. It's a great introduction into the weird world of the primates we saw earlier, called lemurs.

The primary mission of the Ivoloina biological station and wildlife sanctuary is the con-

Lemurs are primates.

Cute little guy, huh?

servation of lemurs, and they're doing this in a variety of ways. One is through outreach and education, and another is through the breeding of endangered species. They're also rehabilitating some rare types of lemurs.

Look at those tails.

There are approximately thirty to thirty-three species of lemurs. The number changes every year, as some species unfortunately become extinct and others are newly discovered. But all the lemurs are found on only one place in the planet, and that is Madagascar. Scientists believe that lemurs first appeared about 55 million years ago, but Madagascar separated from Africa well over 100 million years ago. So, how did the lemurs get here? Some scientists have speculated that ancient primates may have floated here on debris or clumps of vegetation and, over millions of years, evolved into different species of lemurs.

Each species has its own way to survive. Many are specialists, like this eastern bamboo lemur. It's a specialist in that it lives in only one type of habitat, bamboo. It breeds in the bamboo. It eats the bamboo. It's physically designed to crawl and maneuver through thickets of bamboo. So, let's put him back in the bamboo.

Over there is a track to beautiful forest, a good place for finding some wild lemurs.

These lemurs are found nowhere else on Earth.

Bamboo lemur

These lemurs love fruit.

Moving through the canopy above us is a troop of white-fronted lemurs. And as they move through the trees so delicately, like acrobats, they're eating. A variety of fruits makes up the diet of these animals. They love guava and figs. But they'll also eat nectar and tender shoots, and to get a little protein I'm sure they'll partake of an insect or two.

What's neat about this species is that the males and females are very different in appearance. They have the same physical shape, but the females have dark brown fur

The females are darker...

...and the males have white crowns and fronts.

while the males have more of a white crown. The body length is about 15 inches from tip of nose to the base, and they have very long tails.

Look what this male's doing with his foot—he's scratching his head with his back toe. That's a toilet claw—a curved digit and claw that these animals use for grooming. It's a characteristic that's unique to the prosimians.

Using a toilet claw—not a pretty name, but it keeps him pretty.

Most lemurs are active only during the day, but there are some who, like musician Wilson Pickett, prefer the midnight hour. I'm not one who likes to be caged, but for something like this, it's a treat. We're looking at one of the most mysterious of all lemurs, the aye-aye. I have always wanted to see an aye-aye,

Some lemurs only come out at night.

and I would love to see one in the wild, but they're nocturnal and extremely hard to find. They're very secretive, very reclusive.

Large eyes for seeing at night.

Aye-ayes spend much of their lives up in the canopy. They have large eyes for seeing in the darkness, and they have excellent hearing—they can hear the sounds of insects that are foraging inside the tree bark. Here's something else that's very peculiar about these creatures: Their incisors are almost rodentlike, extremely sharp, and they grow throughout this animal's lifetime. The aye-aye uses those powerful incisors to literally chip away at the bark, to sculpt and remove the toughest wood, to get at insects. Then it sticks that long, strange finger in, digs around, pulls the insect out, and eats it.

Large ears to hear the sounds of insects.

There are other lemurs to be found here in Madagascar. One I really want to see is called *Microcebus*, the mouse lemur. To find it, we're going to head to another part of amazing Madagascar.

Pinch me—I can't believe this is happening—I've actually captured a lemur. This is a greater dwarf lemur. The name makes no sense—"greater" and "dwarf"—but that's it. I just grabbed him, and he's not sure what to make of the situation. He's saying, "Please, sir, I didn't do anything wrong. I was just looking for some fruit and some insects. And are you going to eat me?"

I caught this greater dwarf lemur myself!

Look at these feet—almost humanlike.

This creature is one of the smallest types of primates in the world. It is completely nocturnal, more common than the aye-aye but still very difficult to find. Look at the feet—they're almost human-like. Notice how his eyes are set, facing forward, as with most of the primates. That gives him stereoscopic vision—overlapping fields of vision that allow him to judge distances. This depth perception helps him move through branches because it gives him a better understanding of how far away each branch is.

When the times are good and there's lots of food for this animal to eat, he can store 30 percent of his body weight as fat in his tail. That fat serves as a reserve for the times when food is scarce.

Just let your eyes scan this bundle of leaves, and you'll discover that one of these leaves is not like the others. This is a katydid—a grasshopper-like insect that gives new meaning to the word mimic. He is so leaflike that he actually has

All leaves? Or maybe not...

the vein pattern of a leaf. If you look very closely, you can see the central vein going down the middle and the small veins radiating off to the sides.

But wait—there's more. Check out the back end of this creature. His skin, or exoskeleton, is crunched up almost as if he had a

The back end looks like a dying leaf.

Tasting a little Corwin...

disease. But he's perfectly healthy. The dried, frayed skin looks like the end of a dying leaf. There would be no doubt in the eyes and mind of a predator like a chameleon that this creature is nothing but a leaf.

He's nibbling on my fingers. I know I taste very good, but you're a herbivore, my friend. Since I'm not looking for a manicure, let's put this little critter back.

This is one of the many different types of tree frogs in Madagascar. It's a species is unique to this island, the Boophis tree frog.

It has great eyes. They're very much set to the front of this frog's head, to help it see where it's going. And if you look right at the end of this animal's toes, you will see suction discs. Those discs allow the frog to stick to just about anything it crawls upon.

The Boophis tree frog is a suction master.

A very flexible frog...

This animal is extremely flexible for a frog. He can bend his heels and move his head back and forth, which is not the case for many frogs. Just a great little frog.

I just saw a very long and gorgeous snake work its way into some debris....

Look at this—isn't that beautiful? It's a Madagascar hognose snake, and he's just gorgeous. This is one of the longest serpents you'll find in Madagascar. Hognose snakes aren't aggressive, so we can have a real good look at him and see what makes him beautiful.

Why do we call this guy the hognose snake? Look at the end of his muzzle, his rostrum. You can see it is slightly curled up, like a hog's snout. The snake uses his nose like a spade, and he is a master at digging. He digs to excavate himself a little den beneath the debris on the forest floor, or to search for prey.

This is one of the longest snakes in Madagascar.

See his muzzle?

This guy is a frog lover— he loves to eat them.

At the rear of this creature's jaw are two fangs. The snake uses those rear fangs to puncture prey. Why does he need to puncture his prey? This snake loves to eat frogs. When frogs are captured, they bloat up with air, so they're difficult to swallow. How do you swallow that balloon? You pop it. And that's what the snake does with his rear fangs.

I'm going to put this creature back where we found him, and let's continue searching.

Whoa. Look at this—two leaf-nosed snakes, a male and a female. Most of the snakes on Madagascar are not venomous. This is one of the few that are. They're rear-fanged and produce a mild toxin strong enough to take out a small bird, a frog, perhaps a lizard.

Aren't these leaf-nosed snakes the coolest?

What's extraordinary about these serpents is that male and female look like two different species. They're sexually dimorphic, and in snakes that's very unusual. The female is more cryptic—that is, darker in color, with good camouflage for blending in with bark. The male is more vivid. He's got the camouflage in the top; but underneath, his belly is banana yellow.

The tip of the female's nose has a feathery, leaflike shape. The male's nose has a spike-shaped structure, like the toe of an elf

This kind of snake is very sensitive to vibration.

slipper. The leaf-noses of these snakes are very sensitive to vibration. This creature can freeze with its head locked at the end of a branch, looking just like a twig. When a skink or a small chameleon rubs up against that little nose leaf, it triggers a strike response. The snake injects venom into its prey and has a meal.

Now, look at this. It's not a squirrel. It's not chipmunk. It's not a mouse. It is a primate, folks. This is the brown mouse lemur, and it is one of the smallest primates on our planet. In fact, it's probably the smallest primate.

This lemur is one of the smallest primates in the world.

This individual is a sub-adult. At this stage, these creatures are extremely vulnerable because they don't have common sense. They don't know there are predators out there, like snakes and birds of prey. But this little fellow wants to be protected. He's a cavity dweller, and in the daytime you'll find him in a hole.

Those eyes and tiny hands... See the resemblance?

Right now he's sheltering in the palm of my hand.

Human beings share a distant genetic lineage with animals like this. When you look at this creature, with its little fingers and those eyes looking at you inquisitively, you can't help but feel compassion for it. It's living in a part of the world where the habitat is disappearing dramatically, where less than 30 percent of the original habitat remains. What does the future hold for a wonderful thing like this, as well as for the other animals that have evolved so magnificently, so bizarrely, so wonderfully on the island of Madagascar?

I was hoping to find some more creatures here in Madagascar, but to be honest I don't think I can match this discovery. The smallest primate, a brown mouse lemur—it doesn't get any better than this. So, perhaps this is the point where we should wrap up our expedition. I'll see you again on our next adventure!

Glossary

canopy the top layer of a rain forest or kelp forest

conservation preservation or protection

cutaneous respiration breathing through the skin

dimorphic occuring in two distinct forms

ecosystem a community of organisms

endangered species a species whose population is so low it may become extinct

exoskeleton the hard outer covering of an insect or animal

extinct when no more members of a species are alive

foraging wandering and searching for food on the ground

fossils remains of ancient animals found in the earth's crust

habitat a place where animals and plants live naturally together

herbivore an animal that eats plants

insectivore animal that eats insects

mammal a warm-blooded animal that feeds its babies with milk

metabolism processes in the body necessary for life, such as getting energy from food

nectar a sweet liquid produced by some plants

primates types of mammals such as monkeys, apes, or humans

prosimians members of a lower order of primates

rain forest a tropical forest that receives a lot of rain

rehabilitating healing and restoring strength

sanctuary a place where animals are safe and protected

serpents snakes

venomous having a gland that produces poison for self-defense or hunting

Index